Melancolía

Poems

Roberto Carlos Garcia

Červená Barva Press
Somerville, Massachusetts

Copyright © 2016 by Roberto Carlos Garcia

All rights reserved. No part of this book may be reproduced in any manner without written consent except for the quotation of short passages used inside of an article, criticism, or review.

Červená Barva Press
P.O. Box 440357
W. Somerville, MA 02144-3222

www.cervenabarvapress.com

Bookstore: www.thelostbookshelf.com

Cover artist: Roberto Carlos Garcia

Cover design: William J. Kelle

ISBN: 978-0-9981027-1-9

Library of Congress Control Number: 2016955600

Distributed by Small Press Distribution: www.spdbooks.org

ACKNOWLEDGMENTS

I am grateful to the editors of the following publications where these poems first appeared, sometimes in different versions.

Barrelhouse: "A riot in images"

Lunch Ticket: "What can I tell you"

Olentangy Review: A version of "Name it"

pluck! The Journal of Affrilachion Arts & Culture: "Duplicity"

Public Pool: "No currency" and "Savior complex"

The Stillwater Review: "Belief System" and "Reading Rorschach Cards"

Tuesday: An Art Project: "If my name was Yusef Aziz"

Word Peace: A version of "I cannot write anything"

5 AM: "Ars Poetica"

AUTHOR'S NOTE

Melancolía is as easily defined as its elusive cousin, *Duende*. Which is another way of saying it is indefinable. Ancient and medieval physicians believed an excess of one or more of the four primary bodily fluids caused it. I won't bore you with that. You can Google it, or visit a library. I'm more interested in what it does to poets. In the way *melancolía* makes poets long for things that have been, that have yet to pass, and that might have never existed. It makes a poet ache for the beauty and the brevity of life—the fleeting scent and brightness of the rose's many dresses, of spring and summer's shifting heat, and for the childhood that could have been. *Melancolía* is thirst for joy and believe it or not, pain. It is the heat of lust and the shame of lusting, of not being able to have the thing or person you desire. *Melancolía* is pure longing and the restless, depressed and wretched anxiety of longing. And yet it is significantly more complicated than that. We experience *melancolía* physically.

In her essay collection *Sidewalks*, Valeria Luiselli describes the symptoms of *melancolía* as "sadness, crying, stress, headaches, chest pains, insomnia, fatigue, and hallucinations." I'd also add a peculiar unquenchable thirst for wine. These pains must be expressed, poured out, painted, sung, or written. The struggle must be given life. Here is where the evil little cousin *Duende* knocks incessantly at our door. *Melancolía* feeds the monster—it feeds *Duende*. Garcia Lorca wrote, "We only know that he [*duende*] burns the blood like a poultice of broken glass, that he exhausts, that he rejects all the sweet geometry we have learned, that he smashes styles, that he leans on human pain with no consolation..." He also wrote that an old maestro of the guitar told him, "The *duende*, then, is a power, not a work. It is a struggle, not a thought." I take "thought" to mean overthinking, the draining of life from the artistic idea, leaving the body and retiring completely into the mind. Trying to shake off *melancolía*, to shake off the pain or experience that feeds the art.

What then causes *melancolía* in us? What brings on our symptoms? Is it the world's lack of social justice, is it racism, is it war, is it heartbreak, the death of loved ones, the fear of death, the accumulation of perceived slights and offenses, loneliness, unrequited love, unfulfilled desire, the fear of God, of heaven or hell, the lack of courage, poverty, the overwhelming ignorance pervading our world, the endless list of *isms* and phobias, the apocalypse, the death of a rose? How then to express this, to be a poet that masters *melancolía* and the mysterious and dangerous outburst of expression that is *duende*? I don't pretend to know, but I give in to it. I simply enjoy the struggle, the fight to understand. Not thought but contemplation, like a Sufi seeking truth.

This book is a product of what is for me a sacred struggle with *melancolía*.

TABLE OF CONTENTS

No currency	3
Melancolía	5
Whispers	6
This is not an elegy	7
Heal thy self	8
Have moon dreams	9
From my kitchen window	11
Secrets	12
Duplicity	13
Savior complex	14
On a good day	16
ars poetica	17
This body	18
The poem you asked for	19
Name it	20
Self-medicate	21
Self portrait in American black	22
Keeping on	24
Melancolía	25
What can I tell you	26
You just have to play it by ear, and pray for rain	27
Drive	28
At dinner	29
Whiskey prayer	30
Mirror	31
Blood cake	32
The apocalypse up close	33
I cannot write anything	36
In white silence	37
A riot in images	38
If my name was Yusef Aziz	39
Anchorite	40
Forms of tenderness	41
I gave Emily Dickinson to you then	42
Belief system	43
Reading Rorschach cards	44
Traffic	45
There is my mountain	46

Clean	47
This is an elegy	48
Toil	49
A poet is a nightingale who sits in darkness and sings	50
ars poetica	51

Notes
Thanks and Praise
About the Author

There is no such thing as a nostalgic or *"saudadic"* child, but there are melancholy ones.

>—Valeria Luiselli,
>"Alternate Routes"

The weight of the world
      is love.
Under the burden
      of solitude,
under the burden
      of dissatisfaction

      the weight,
the weight we carry
      is love.

— Allen Ginsberg, "Song"

Melancolía

No currency

My loveseat in suburbia is distance
between me & the world beyond the flat screen,
a world I'd love to crush like a dictator,
a sad dictator,

El Generalissimo Ridiculissimo,
for this world where children burn

like the dry bush of California countryside,
where firefighters come to save the houses, & die

From my loveseat in suburbia
as useful as a clown's nose—

After all, who can afford water?

I'm a father of three, growing fat Meanwhile
hunger is killing nations / gluttony is killing nations,
I wear floppy feet

but as *El Generalissimo,* I will complete the carnage,
the crazy complicity

Ah, poets!

We are one & the same—rabble what you rabble

Divine a poem,
or a poet, for that matter

What you imply is fireworks,
but the truth is empty wine bottles

Water is made clear by the current,
if it be hell say it is hell

From my loveseat in suburbia, I do nothing,
but *El Generalissimo* can instigate metamorphosis

Kids, what should we turn into / what will become of us?
Pass me the remote control

Melancolía
      —after Giorgio De Chirico's *Melancholia*, 1916

At times I feel broad like shadows in a courtyard,
or insignificant, a faraway speck squinting from the moon,

I am obsessed,
but without an object

Husband, father, son—
but in the sun I cry easily,
like a child lamenting a fallen ice cream cone,
the fine line between caring & catatonia,
dust in a sun ray

I self-medicate—wine
until the questions become clear

I suppose the symmetry of fresh-cut lawns,
polished cars, & opposing driveways
is the only dunce cap I can wear,
my flag in the wind & I don't believe in it

A nun, Sister Elizabeth, taught me a song:
she says she's holding out hope for me:

This is the day the Lord has made
Let us rejoice and enjoy it

It's in my head as I count the tchotchkes
listen to trains in the distance,
& wander from light to dark
between the rooms in my house

Whispers

The wind outside my window is doubt:
it reminds me that words are insufficient,

that we can only remake the past as lies,
so I promise never to dream in pencil again;
I will paint red, blue, & green oil memories,

letters textured like toothpaste

I will prick all ten fingertips & paint in blood,
even if the words
don't promise to last any longer

How do the evergreens in my yard stand immortality,
the wind coaxing their needles to fall?

I warn my kids: *Be careful. They're pointy. You'll bleed*:
who'll keep me tethered here?

Words, pencils, oils, & blood—
I'm carrying on
All things dance their way to dust,
but I must stay here

Let's refuse
Come leap through the keyhole with me:
don't open the door

Behind my window dreams are better without permission:
there's no wind to wipe the canvas white again

This is not an elegy

This is not an elegy, but I was haunted,
mesmerized by how ablaze leaves are in death,
the yellow red browns scattered across my lawn
& I felt my little sister sitting there
she's been gone six years now—
felt her caress like autumn winds
the kind that don't go back empty-handed,
& I believed in spring resurrection,
but the leaves cried like poppy fields
& she floated away

Autumn's ruse, the artifice
of leaves falling from trees—
I can't name it

Heal thy self

There's some Confucian wisdom in paper cuts,
in allegedly harmless things & carelessness,

that we are naked as glass is naked,
blind like sunlight in what we burn,
pebbles hurled callously shattering worlds

I watch a few bumblebees stick their long hairy tongues
deep into the heads of blooming rose beds

How delicious to drink & be sated by such beauty,
to forget what ties me to the animal world,
mortgages, & hard swallows

Let's name each other according to our birthmarks

I want to live like the nectar from a rose—
warm river inside the withering reds & yellows—
to live like nectar carried off by the bumblebees,
a little spilled here, a little pissed there

Have moon dreams
    —after Miles Davis

I hear the crag sound
of trash dragged
down cold ashen asphalt

I check the lock on the door,
go to the kitchen window
where moonlight's bath softens
a praying wind's *Diana, Diana,*

& the whole yard's bright as daytime
The trees, grass, & houses
under a chrome bulb

Moon, every many-legged thing
from my nightmares praises you tonight,

a raucous pagan feast
of strangeness in the shadows

Sleepless moon-silver night,
only dawn quiets the exhausted revelry

Moon, drunk in a burning sky,

shining out of agony,
reigning over a bit of time,

& foolish lovers moan
in moonlight dripping
through midnight's blinds

We are drawn to the moon
like animals baffled
at their own reflections

The hunter's moon,
an overripe grapefruit sticky

& oozing a luminous liquor

I kneel open-mouthed swallowing
air but the moon refuses to fall;

it goads me, a bending branch
pretending to break
as my tongue & throat beg & pray

& the sea inside me
riots for release

Full moon lullaby,
Diana, Diana

I walk with her under an April moon:
she doesn't speak;

my tongue trembles
at the sight of the nearing woods
& the scent of spring lovemaking in the night

She smiles and smiles

I follow

From my kitchen window

I heard spring speak against summer—
Only birth is beautiful:
to live is to struggle
& die everyday

I was washing dishes
when summer spoke against autumn—
She dresses death so lovely,
so many layers of color
& decay

I was surprised to hear
Autumn praise winter—
I would give anything to see it,
but in the end we fall face down,
brown as tree trunks

Again I waited
but winter said nothing—
silent as a starless sky above a grave,

like a birth cry
angry at life,
a red-orange death dream,
a ghost watching the world fade—

Secrets

Secrets hide over the skin—
like ivy growing on brick

I must touch my way out of them,
use my tongue, knees & elbows

wave as I cross
the crumbling bridge,

the patchwork stairs,
& leap, eyes shut & heart wide

in the waterfall & downriver into an ocean
of feet & dirt,

then beg forgiveness
for not telling you—

Keeping secrets means
crawling on all fours in pain,
strutting proud in a pair of new shoes,

praying facedown in the mud, ass in the air,
out of shame

Duplicity

Hard truth:

First thing I do
as I breathe into a room
is search
for brown & black faces,
bobbing in America's
post racial waters

I swim peripheral glances
Back-stroke being ignored
Wade on a chair
in a corner of the room
& chat up the Help

until,

some(not brown or black)one
tosses me
an integration life-
line

Hard truth:

Light & Dark
sparkle the waters
like tinsel,
pretty chimera

No one really
has to

Does anyone *really*
have to?

Talk to me—

Savior complex

1.

Kneel & make salāt five times a day

If the world knew what birds know of love—
each one of you could be part of me

Think how many could be saved
I too am able to watch the world burn
from a deck in the woods, a drink in my hand

We believe that's okay

2.

Supplicate the Father, the Son & the Holy Spirit

I agree about wine, bread, & olives—vespers
I'll hold hands with you,
& we'll listen to one another's pain

The love between us a peace accord,
an oasis in hell, a dream temple
we enter asleep, only

3.

Say ten Hail Marys—look around—repeat

On my knees I pretend to be a tsunami
washing away the suffering—
resurrecting the damned from the sea as clouds

My hands in adulation: *Up there*, I say *Look up there!*
The meek shall inherit fresh ink,
& Earth shall inherit a new story

You & I must continue to pray

4.

Give zakat to the poor & needy

I can no longer make a fist—neither to hit nor to hide things
I hear fire redeems best
My friends, I am not above you—

I can hear the song of reckoning in the rose thorns

On a good day

I skip down avenues
of endless green traffic lights—

In my navel a supernova,
my sex a cloud nebulae,
my mouth a black hole

The cosmos is inside me:
I fall in love every day

because the distance between love
& madness is an eyelash,
the tip of a goose-bump down to the flesh

Take my nakedness:
wear it over your shirt like a vest—

bring me yellow suns;
bring me every human;

        we'll be comet—ice, tail, & dust—
        we'll fly off the edge of this earth we've flattened—

ars poetica
    —after Rilke

Did I forget to open my eyes back there,
to breathe with my heart,
& to carry all the hope I can
in my lungs?

I would sing—I would, & dance all the time,
but if this apathy was human
I'd murder too

Wind flips the weathervane:
only three blue jays, hunting in the rain
approach with any light

My beautiful friend says,
The doctor put me on a wine diet—
you should try it,
& I see light for a little while:
I ride shotgun in another's dreams

My pen longs to be paintbrush, glamorous quill,
& my resolve, well—
to write is to seek beauty,
to give the world hope

I prefer the openmouthed kiss
of simple devastation

Blame morbidity
trampling the roses within me

Enough about that; tell me how *you* are
Write back quickly

One last note; things are dire;
please send money

This body

My world dangles
on a wisp of spider web,

knees ache & knuckles pop,

& wet or hard,
hunger is a bicep flexing,
a madness for heat & touch
so natural its breath is dirt

Pray God breaks the fever,
run an ice cube from your breast
to your navel,

drip the cold on your sex,
for all the good it will do you

The poem you asked for

I watched a white heron alight on a lake
& turned the image into another,
of my soul departing from heaven
as a mustard seed on a river of blood

I don't know why I go there,
my body—lost in the wild hunger of skin,
free from an ether I can no longer feel—
groping breathing suffering

I ache for sensation,
for cold nights under starlight
& hot showers

Perhaps a truth about me will rise
from the crusted muddy surface of this poem

I care what you think of it,
but within measure;
you asked for a poem—now here I am
naked & throbbing on the page

Name it

So I went for a walk,
playing at shamelessness
in broad daylight, pulled left
by the weight of hope's starry imagination,

& the sun was still out,
gold strings on a guitar,

& it sounded so cotton candy,
felt so salty, tasted so transient

I was trying to hear God in the birdsong,
to be favored like Solomon
without the drama

I wonder if that's greed,
melancholy capriciousness,
or what the philosophers called
human frailty

Self-medicate

I'm keeping the moon in a mason jar with wine;
when it shines at a right angle I swig
openmouthed, belch sparks, nuzzle deeper
into the soil's shoulder, into a bed of dead leaves,
& pray it all catches fire

Then I'll be an ember on a blazing landscape—
I'll be like the stars

Self portrait in American black
>   *(for the silent)*

I am that I am—what America TV's me;
>   monstrous chameleon,
>   schizophrenic Janus,

transformed, transmuted—
>   switching black image
>   for your mind's white eye / I

I line up the game winner:
>   *Shoot it!*
>   I stand arms raised

I am on the corner:
>   *Don't shoot!*
>   I stand arms raised

>   the crowd gives a standing ovation

I stand mic in hand, arms raised:
>   *I am a god, now hurry up wit my damn massage!*
>   the crowd sings along

I am unseen—I am conjured:
>   I am that I am the entertainment
>   you seek when you need
>   to dance
>   to sport
>   to laugh
>   to cry
>   to feel like God

I am that I am what
>   America's narrative makes me:
>   A STRUGGLE ENSUES,
>   A BRIEF ALTERCATION,
>   & I stand as death's bride

arms raised—arms wide,
    black play-doh
        for your mind's white eye / I

Keeping on

—an American sonnet, after Gerald Stern

Morning cold is worst, rising from the ground
& grabbing at old ankle & knee injuries;
the new day opens like a horrific crash
I can't look away from, & the hope
that there are survivors becomes the thing
dragging me to the shower & hot water;
the steam makes me think of coffee,
dark & deep like the sleep I long to return to;
I step out to the second cold, dry off slowly;
life's conveyor belt accelerates; now it's about
keeping up, as the little voice grows louder
& louder until I'm sitting in the car, weighing
all the options, the infinite variations of doubt,
& what scares me most is not sitting still
but careening through space & time decaying
as quickly as the paths I choose not to travel,
& the voice grows louder, familiar from yesterday
& the day before, going so far back there's no point
looking—I listen as the voice becomes a song,
obey it, close my eyes, & give thanks

Melancolía

> *Walk into my cage and ask the lions*
> *—Frank Lima*

In my mouth melancolía is an orchard,
a yellowing day & bluing night

In my ribcage melancolía is an ecstatic lilt
made of pearls, my heart—wet sand,
pungent as dogwoods

In the graveyard of my head,
in the lion's mouth salty & wet,

in the endless paso doble
of my lungs—melancolía

In the absence, the nothingness,
the lean parched tongue of longing,
in the winding along a cobble stone path

in this desolate garden,
in my voice unheard, choked by dirt,
in the secret of dew
& scent of rebirth downwind
melancolía

In weeping sorrowful or joyful tears,
in lying here among the animals,

on my knees in my fear of God,
through my doubts in fatherhood,
in feasting & drinking, in starving,
during nightmares & dreams,
in passion & apathy,
in life & death & in between—

melancolía

What can I tell you
           —an ars poetica

I confess
from you I learned
sweat is poison as well as nectar,

& there is no good word
for how I linger as you exhale

I confess
I am a cracked mirror,
& you are a stone, a bird,
starlight tickling the fractures

From you I learned jilting
doesn't require stepping away

I confess
I drink your furious glow
like the color black,
like a poet

whose mouth is a bucket,
whose head is an ocean of roses

You just have to play it by ear, and pray for rain
—James Baldwin

My guardian angel is tired,
the crick in her neck a pinched nerve
that makes her fingers numb;

she's ready for bright velour jumpsuits
& Crocs

I push life I push it like I know I'm protected

My friend called me,
dreamed he was at my funeral

Happens all the time, I said:
I'm not peeking around corners,

jerking my head to the cardinal points
I wonder about replacements though;

perhaps I'll write a love poem
& woo a new guardian angel

I feel like I ate too much cornbread
& forgot to ask for a drink

Hear my prayer, Lord:
this life is a mirror in a lightning storm,
a trumpet solo on a splintered stage,

a footrace against a faster man,
a child picking daffodils

Before I start my prayer, tell me,
are angels really androgynous?

Drive

I'm listening to Vampire Weekend
on my drive home, & I wouldn't know
what a Vampire Weekend is except
that my daughter made me a playlist
for my fortieth birthday; & I'm grateful
we listen to so much music together,
because I can't stop dancing to this track,
track three, & I'm maybe speeding a little
thinking of how fast the years pass & come
up on you at the same time; & then I see
the biggest blackest raven you'd ever want
to see, pecking the red pulpy roadkill
of some poor beast too slow to swim life's
wave & there's nothing left but the strips
of its insides, & the raven's having its fill,
& isn't that the mystery? & if life isn't a road
you speed down, looking periodically
in the rearview as the houses, trees, people
& places whiz by, & if life isn't eating your
red pulpy guts at the same time as you eat
life's indigestible flesh, dancing, singing even
to a song full of sentiment, then we're doing it
wrong, I'm doing it wrong, & please tell me
what is more real than the peck-peck-peck
of devouring this life

At dinner

Maybe the woman I drew in blue crayon—

The children & I shared a green & a blue one,
doodled on the tablecloth; we chattered,
ate bread, waited for entrées, celebrated
Gramms birthday

The couple next to us tried discreetly
to study my blue woman, passed along
their awkwardness (the woman, sad),
stared into each face at our table—
the man, silent, as if to say,
Don't be so obvious

She made me uncomfortable:
when our food arrived,
she watched us devour it

After—the bus boy took our dishes
I studied the sad woman, the indifferent man;
He rose,
went to the bathroom without excusing himself;
she didn't notice, drank wine instead of noticing,

& I thought I saw her memories & tragedies,
their emptiness on the legs of the wine & even after;
when we were leaving, my wife's uncle asked me
if I'd noticed her pale skinned Eastern European features,
her elegance   I remarked how she appeared sullen;
he replied he hadn't noticed that

Whiskey prayer

Piety is weak thunder in the face of cocksure lightning:
pray for a life like falling stars;
pray the cool rain of sin makes the soul saintly

A prophet's tale is a lyric once you've heard the blues:
I'm stroking the silk between worlds:
a shaman should know as many souls as places

Blood in a cup is strange magic
if you've bled your own

Mirror

White hairs sprout on my face & head—

I enjoy wasting time:
I'm always looking back,
unraveling the years like a lemon peel

I remember friends at points in time
like a necklace of Cheerios on a piece of fuzzy yarn

I miss my friends, all of them,
even as far back as I cannot remember

These days my face in the mirror is a brown galaxy—
I am becoming more earth than man

Blood cake
> *poems with no lilies or moons / and no love affairs about to fail*
> —Federico García Lorca

The earth is a blood cake

Blood bubbling in the soil, in the sea,
dripping from the skies

Blood stretching in the wheat, the corn;
blood crackling in the rice fields

The colors on my palette,
red, yellow, black, brown, white—
herein is the world,

& yet blood means a man, a woman, a child

No crust, magma, or core,
only blood crying out
from the subconscious
of every living thing

Mother Earth will come calling

In the lakes, rivers, & oceans of blood,
in the fields, hills, & mountains of blood,
each rose, sunrise, & sunset;
blood limp in a champagne glass,

a toast to

    the tin taste

        of blood

            in the cake

The apocalypse up close

1.

I tremble in a strange column

I hold a weapon (a sword, a gun, a bomb, poison,
words,) & the rest of this regiment—

brothers, daughters, grandmothers, & sick people—
all carry the weapon; black, white, gay,

straight, yellow, red, we number in the millions—
At the head of each column a captain

reads from the Bible, the Koran, the Talmud, a book of poems
& froths at the mouth for theater

There is doom in the air, thirst at the back of our throats;
in our mouths we know we must kill—

we are scared, weeping aimless tears;
we name our weapons: *Apathy, Dissatisfaction*

Banners convulse in a half wind, & we stand
on a beach of salt & iron,

to our right a rock wall, to our left the sea full of orcas,
across from us another army

full of people I know & a cry rising,
the petty grievances of the apocalypse:

He denied me a plate of food:
She wouldn't sleep with me:
He never listened to my advice:
She was more successful—
More beautiful,
He broke my heart:
He's not a believer—

Never took me seriously:
An ass kisser:
She's a racist:
He's an Uncle Tom:
She never calls me back:

Only the bugle, loud as a skyscraper
crumbling calls us to action

We charge, the weapon firing
slight & deliberate pain—

I recognize my loved ones,
& they recognize me,

but we tear flesh from limb anyway,

& with each death the sea is roiling, a flood
of blood & guilt hardening sand to cement, the killing

so difficult many die while killing,
hearts give out, aneurisms burst

We're like butchers—bloody gut water up to
our chins, until we drown choking on each other

2.

No taking five, people
How did it apocalypse?
We lived the long way around,

reneged mercy & sympathy,
defaulted the world flat again,
disproved everything

Time now for reckoning;
no slogans, jingles, or yellowing
the cosmos happy-as-fuck-it

We plead not guilty, apocalypse—
we redeem our acts;
the world was our stage, not our fault

We reject adjudication (while rubbing
at the dry blood on our skin,) but it clings
like the will to live, or some smell,

& the executioner walks in
humming a tune, turns to us:
If you can wash off the blood, you're forgiven
He buckets water on us:
the more we wash, the bloodier
we get, red then oily black,

& we drown in blood again,
another death, a darker night,
being crushed in the mouth of an orca

We scream we will come out clean
on the other side; we hear
the executioner shout, *No chance*

3.

We repent! We repent;
it's dark down here We
repent; we can't see or smell
We repent! We repent;

our form is formless We
repent; we can't believe this We
want a cold one, a smoke!
We repent! For God's sake,

isn't that what we're supposed to say?

I cannot write anything
—Czeslaw Milosz

I despair for the world,
its hunger, violence, & corruption—
Suffocating

in pitiless noise drowning out pleas,
poetry weakens
I cannot write anything

Poetry wants images, metaphors—

I refuse the reader redemption:
I tell it miserably & you will taste iron in the blood—
I drag you in
I cannot write anything

Hissing drones lurking in the skies:
The fathers of dead children don't cry, they wail
I defy poetry I rant

Poetry misfires
I want bullet wounds, bomb blasts, & tears on the page:
Howl with me,

forsake everything;
Here is your crown of thorns—
A starving child like an open gash

faces turn from on the street
I cannot write anything

What is poetry that does not try to save nations or people?

What are people who do not read such poetry?
Whatever poetry does—
I cannot write anything

In white silence

America remains a matchstick;
a bundle of dry-wood—kerosene

I POST a STATUS,
you LIKE & COMMENT, but

we're just mouthing;
a script unfolds, a TV special,

& all the while black bodies—dandelions
breaking in quiet breezes

Our black bodies—dust peeling
off America's skin—

swept from a street corner,
a Wal-Mart, a park—our black bodies

dumped in Object, Other, Thing

A cold autumn day of white silence
of one minute a friend & the next   a space

a loyalty strange as strange fruit,
a privilege like air through teeth

White sister, brother,
I cannot make you feel

I paint the portrait
I *danse macabre*

I disintegrate in front of you, but
in white silence—there aren't even shadows

A riot in images

A hooded sweatshirt
hung upside down,
flag at half-mast

A cop huffs & puffs a teen down a city street:
one's running scared, one's running fast;

two hearts buck, one heart blown away
like a sandcastle in a storm

Weary eyes weep, observe
a void in a torso & another   *another*

Wooly black hair bloody
sponge matts the pavement

A dragon tail of white black & brown faces,
a cop searing like a conifer tree
in centuries-old-fire

Ash falls on lips & tongues, ash on eyelids—
heaps of ash from the reckoning;

bricks melt like butter in the sun;
people melt like ice in rum

Mercy   Mercy   Mercy
water on cracked bleeding lips

If my name was Yusef Aziz

First a little history; I'm a three
twined rope—the oldest of which
is like fine hair from a baobab tree
in sunny bush; & the second oldest
like rabbit tails— a fuzzy cord
slippery to the grip; & the last is chain
greased with bloody pulpy conquest;
I study this rope; I study me; & so say
my name doubting it is a true name,
& as the rope is aging only the strongest
twine doesn't feather but smells of earthy
sap; it permeates every vein, relentless,
& now a little sorcery—my skin belongs
to a continent, my name to a conquistador,
& this howling greedy spirit to a nation
just two centuries old, & could I change that
by conjuring or reinventing or rebranding
or rebirth or renewal or renouncing, yes,
renouncing, & I renounce you;
get thee behind me name that doesn't match
my baobab twine hair, skin, & song,
& now a little sacrifice—some for you, some for me;
don't you call me by that other name;
use only this new one I had to make
magic & piss copper to steal back

Anchorite

Mornings I read the dew drops on my windshield
like an old *santero* fortune-telling
from a coffee cup & still I speak
my prayers into the world's mouth

because

Forms of tenderness

There's anger in baby pictures
stretched boys & girls on city stoops

As I run I go faster & hope that faster
means I'm leaving more behind;
Tell me again about relativity,
tell me about shooting stars
It's about ignoring the thorn,
but the pain isn't mine, I run
so others can let go
No looking back, no piles of salt,
only footsteps, soft phone calls,
& urns full of regrets
Regrets fall best like sweat in the rain
Run—make distance a stand-in for memory
Make suffering a form of tenderness

I gave Emily Dickinson to you then
—Agha Shahid Ali

as if she were a cold or
a lasting heirloom,
a piece of my living soul

So dangerous to make woman metaphor
though I prefer to call her sea, ocean
All the mountains & hills removed

Emily,
is there room at your small wooden desk
for the waters & me?

I will hold your dress one-handed in the wind:
we'll take turns writing slant rhymes,
our feet gritty with sea salt,

my tongue a barn swallow
full of slang,
your eyes foam, black waves

I gave you, Emily,
to keep you;
this is how I love,

so I can rise
from your desk, your ocean,
soaked in lady slipper orchids

Belief system

I believe in the magic of kissing,
of low-cut dresses, too much wine,
& slow dancing

I believe you will be remembered
by how you make love,
& that loving is the best way
to know one another

I believe water was turned
into wine; it makes sense;
I wish I could've been there

I believe we are all mustard seeds,
yellow as stars & just as perilous
I believe we should rename ourselves—

I believe I love to the point of being
an imbecile,
then shrink like tissue

When I weep like this everyone hates me

Reading Rorschach cards

Fine white dust on a loaf of bread
Broken heart pounding in a lunch pail
Crooked crumbling concrete steps
Sunshine rolling 'round a wind-filled sail
Mother mending socks & underpants
Trees creaking in a moonlit wind
Rolled up trousers—winemaker's dance
Pins & needles, needles & pins
Leather shoes, leather belt, leather jacket
Crimson, ocher, cobalt, & umber fingernails
The night makes the aura, & the J can't hack it
Silver trail along a lane of slimy snails

A giant box of painted wooden toys
Birthday boy, birthday boy, birthday boy

Traffic

This poem takes place in traffic,
the traffic of bills at a set time every month,
of people, obstacles, & the self inflicted

I went to pick up my little adjunct check,
wove through the traffic of red tape & slack

On my way home I sat in traffic
Stuck under the overpass I saw a pack of men
on the sidewalk blocking people traffic,

back & forth around a cardboard box,
like mall traffic, circulating
A man rose from the box & another took his place

I checked the clock; could I beat traffic to the bank
Everyone's rubbernecking, we see knees & feet,
hiked above the cardboard box & a man squatting,

& then last week's memory of a woman sulking,
        (in the same chair)
looking / scanning & now she's on the ground,
under a man who'll stand & walk off into traffic

A father crossed the street with his daughter
to circumvent the traffic made up of clots blocking

us up or laying us down in the guts of a box;
the traffic of set bills at a set time every month

or the rumble of a lack of traffic in our guts,
or the traffic of the next fix,
or just because there's too much traffic
& we want out

There is my mountain

There is my mountain,
a slim volume of poems
facedown in a rain puddle

I have no coat, no scarf,
& a beggar making fire says to me,
Bring the book—let's burn it

& what is poetry if not what we need?

Clean

The leaf blower does its work with ease,
& I'm reminded of dead skin or dust
in the corners of the house & how
our human bodies resemble the universe,
the heart like an engine, a star spreading
blood through a galaxy of flesh
I dig a hole with my hands pretending
to make a woman from the fresh
topsoil, the cilantro, & tomatoes,
these hands like a hunk of asteroid—
full of taking & giving, of friend & foe
kneeling in stubborn grass—like a little boy

I know the universe is within this body
& that somewhere along the way I forgot it

This is an elegy
                    —*for Kyana*

I thought I saw your face in the water,
so I followed flickering starlight down the pier,
jumping over the missing boards, wanting to go farther
The bartender called to me, *Okay out there?*
& I lost you in the white foam crashing below
On the sand I decided to roll up my pants & try again
The moon was steady then, & the sea wasn't cold,
just warm the way love is warm—I heard you calling
The bartender touched my back—*The sea,* he warned,
is the road between this world & the next—
he offered me a drink—*I've seen many handsome men called*

by the other side He had the bottle in his pocket
We sat down & got drunk in the water

Toil

My head against yours & I'm falling asleep;
the smell of your shampoo does that,
but I can't stop thinking about the lawn
& why I can't make grass grow on the dead parts;
my heart palpitates, signs of stress, no wine
tonight—too sleepy; & today was hot
& full of work in the yellow heat of a gift
of a day to remind us that yes, summer is real,
& then I look for a metaphor,
some device to explain my tiredness in the face
of such a happy event as an eighty-degree day,
perhaps raking the dead soil or sweeping
the neighbor's cigarette butts
or avoiding eye contact with *that* neighbor—
the one who called my yard ghetto, anonymously,
in a letter left in my mailbox, & then I realize
I miss the hood, the ghetto, the block, whatever;
sure, it was work, life & death work, but true,
what-life-is-about true—survival; & what this
has to do with the parched state of my lawn
I'm afraid to admit because it's too easy to work
hard against something while telling yourself
you're working to achieve it; & honestly
I sleep pretty good at night, but my toil,
so far as the green grass of neatly manicured
lawns, has been for naught; & that shit, my love,
along with wanting the neatly manicured lawn
& the "friendly" approval of neighbors,
contains the mystery that haunts me

A poet is a nightingale who sits in darkness and sings

—Percy Bysshe Shelley

I smell the rain before it rains,
my bones make excellent ears,
& simply my friends,
time has given me grizzle

I hear melancolía calling—
a long-distance relative
I'd rather ignore, but still
I'm curious to know if she sleeps
naked or not

I see I've lived in a rush,
making every endeavor a quickie
I am a drop of water falling
from a cloud made of too little time

Oh God, oh mysterious in the air God,
in that moment before I dream,
before I cum,
before I say, "I am resigned,"
before I put pencil to paper,

I imagine myself in the void
It is dark—a lover's nape—
familiar, yet foreign—always new
It is there that I wait for answers

ars poetica
      —*after García Lorca*

If nothing else it
    must be beautiful

Rebellion;
like Miles Davis' *Sketches of Spain,*

or pearl-topped street lamps
against green-brown trees,
green-blue grass against satin
mists of autumn sky so gray

birds flitting through
    it make silent black & white movies,

or Thursday half-moon sighing,

    against two feet floating free,
no boundaries; *Duende*

like shards of colored glass
    shattered along a winding path,

catching bits of moonlight
    in beautiful rebellion

NOTES

The following epigraphs & poem titles come from the poems and authors below:

1. **Blood cake** *poems with no lilies or moons / and no love affairs about to fail* Federico Garcia Lorca

2. *You just have to play it by ear, and pray for rain.* Spoken by James Baldwin, in a 1961 interview with Studs Terkel.

3. *I gave Emily Dickinson to you then,* from the Agha Shahid Ali poem "A Nostalgist's Map of America"

4. *I cannot write anything* and the line *What is poetry that does not try to change nations or people?* from the Czeslaw Milosz poem "In Warsaw"

5. **Reading Rorschach cards** *The night makes the aura, & the J can't hack it* is a line from the A Tribe Called Quest song "Midnight"

6. *A poet is a nightingale who sits in darkness and sings* is from "A Defence of Poetry" by Percy Bysshe Shelley

The first "Melancolía" poem is inspired by "Melancolía" a painting by Giorgio di Chirico.
http://www.moma.org/collection/artist.php?artist_id=1106

THANKS AND PRAISE

Bismillāhi rahmāni rahīm—All gratitude & reverence to the almighty God, The Most Gracious, the Most Merciful.

Thanks & praise to my wife & kids for sacrificing time with me, so that I can write. & my mother in law for holding it down while I'm at the dining room table writing. The biggest sacrifice is always time. I love y'all more than you will ever know.

Thanks & praise to my grandmother for her unconditional love & my mom for the gifts & the genes & the lessons on how to be a man, & my aunt Judy—I know you'll keep a copy of this safely hidden away & bust it out when I least expect it. & Josh, Jordon—Gabby & the kids, Billy, Chantel, and Xavier. I love y'all.

Thanks & praise to my Martin Street brothers, Victor Marzo, Luis Colon, Massimo Galarza, Diego & David Dominguez, Leo Zuniga, Gianni Migliaccio, Eddie Rios, Glen Roy Richards Jr, Sandra, Chris, & the whole fam. Mad love.

Thanks & praise to my Get Fresh Crew: **Darla Himeles** for reading this manuscript mad times & for pick pick picking through it like a boss at a firm, **Peter Kirn** for reading it like a scholar & affording it mad respect—Wilkinson! Brown water & pipes!, **Yesenia Montilla** for believing in me & looking at me sideways when I didn't believe in me & for your honesty & for always stopping to eat Mamoun's falafel with me at the end of the night! & for 30 / 30s!, **Brett Haymaker** for the talks & the friendship & the inspiration & for being my brother & for jumping on countless flights to be here when we need you, **Sean Morrissey** for being my roommate throughout Drew! & that week in Baltimore & for your example & for being Sean Morrissey (woke as fuck), **Lynne McEniry** for always being a phone call away & for all the selfless love you carry for all of us & for your postcards, **Mary Brancaccio** for your heart & for how much you care & for listening, really listening, **Sosha Pinson** for your twang & for writing poems that set me on fire & for being a soldier deep, deep down inside, **Cara Armstrong** for the kiss that saved my life one night & for your tenderness, **Heidi Sheridan** for your impromptu Face Time calls!

& for always reaching out & smiling through it all & for saying California stuff!, **Marisa Frasca Patinella** for laughing & dancing & drinking & fighting with me & for this twinkly eyes, **Shaun Fletch Fletcher** for the greatest introduction anyone has ever given me at a poetry reading "Muck bucket!" & for your humility & your ginormous heart, **Lisa Alexander** for your Pittsburgh swag & how it infects your poems & how real you are doing what you gotta do! Mad love crew, mad mad love.

Thanks & praise to my Drew MFA alums—it's all about the work! Ysabel Gonzalez, Caelen "Tree" Treacy, Bruce Lowry, Anique Taylor (& Misha!), Cindy Snow, Gail Langstroth, Michael Bross, Michelle Greco, Chelsea Palermo, Derek Kelly, Dylan Cecchini, Monica Hand, Rebecca Gayle Howell, Taylor Rickett, James Spears, Kristin Leskowitz, Jane Seitel, Elliott Batzadek, Marta Lucia Vargas, Kathy Engle, Jude Laure Denis, Lori Wilson, Karen Malzone, Fadel Jaber, Miriam Starc, Anu Mahadev, Rick Carter, & on & on & on!

Thanks & praise to the critical & honest eyes, ears, hearts & minds of Rebecca Gayle Howell—thanks for your commitment to supporting your fellow poets & for your honest words about this manuscript, Tamara Hart—thanks killah—you're next!, Ann Davenport—thank you for reading everything I write!, Jesse Burns—quiet genius & razor sharp humor!, Debbie Kuan via Brooklyn Poets mentoring & workshops.

Thanks & praise to Anne Marie Macari for inviting me into her home to just talk about this manuscript & always responding to my emails & for the sacred feminine & for Drew—you've done a wonderful thing—so much more than you'll ever know—I am so grateful. & thank you Gerald Stern for the songs, the stories, & for that wonderful day @ Riverside Park in NYC.

Thanks & praise to my mentors, teachers, & friends Aracelis Girmay, Ross Gay, Judith Vollmer,
Alicia Ostriker, Ellen Dore Watson, Michael Waters, Patrick Rosal, Mihaela Moscaliuc, Jane Mead, Ira Sadoff & Sean Nevin.

Thanks and praise to Anson Pope, for reading all those awful early poems.

Thanks & praise to all the venues where I read these poems. In particular: Allison Geller & Melissa Ahart @ Roots Reading Series in Brooklyn NY, Cynthia Manick @ Soul Sister Revue in NYC, Sean Nevin @ Drew University MFA Program, Marina Careirra @ Brick City Speaks in Newark NJ, Martin Farawell @ The Dodge Poetry Foundation, CeCe Falls @ OPEN Expression in Harlem, The New York City Poetry Festival, Bridgette Davis & Rob Fields @ Sundays@ Reading Series in Brooklyn, NY, Stephen Langlois @ BREW: An Evening of Literary Works, Brooklyn, NY.

Thanks & praise for the tireless & amazing Gloria Mindock. Thank you for believing in my work & for publishing my book!

ABOUT THE AUTHOR

Roberto Carlos Garcia's chapbook *amores gitano* (gypsy loves) was published by Červená Barva Press in 2013. His poems and prose have appeared or are forthcoming in *Public Pool, Stillwater Review, Gawker, Barrelhouse, Tuesday; An Art Project, The Acentos Review, Lunch Ticket, Bold As Love Magazine, Entropy, PLUCK!: The Journal of Affrilachian Arts & Culture, The Rumpus, 5 AM, Wilderness House, Connotation Press- An Online Artifact, Poets/Artists, Levure Litteraire*, and others. Roberto also works with The Dodge Poetry Foundation's poetry in the classroom program. He is the founder of Get Fresh Books LLC: a cooperative press.

Melancolía is his first book.

A native New Yorker, Roberto holds an MFA in Poetry and Poetry in Translation from Drew University, and is an Instructor of English at Union County College.

His website is www.robertocarlosgarcia.tumblr.com.

CPSIA information can be obtained
at www.ICGtesting.com
Printed in the USA
BVOW04s1714160517
484257BV00001B/7/P